10 Tough Little Tigers

Written by **Norma Kaub**

Illustrated by **Beth Snider**

10 Tough Little Tigers

Copyright © 2022, 1999 by Norma Jean Kaub.

All rights reserved. No part of this work may be reproduced or transmitted in any form or by any means, electronic or mechanical, including photocopying and recording, or by any information storage or retrieval system, except as may be expressly permitted by the 1976 Copyright Act or in writing from the publisher.

ISBN (hardcover): 979-8-9867166-0-2
ISBN (softcover): 979-8-9867166-1-9

Cover and interior design by Marisa Jackson for TLC Book Design, TLCBookDesign.com.

3 Tough Little Tigers run, jump, and play.

Making This Book Interactive

Each line or phrase within this book has two parts:

    1) A showing of fingers for the number of tigers, and
    2) A showing of the actions of the tigers..

A child watches and listens as you hold up the appropriate number of fingers (one, two, three, etc) while saying and doing the motions in the same beat as the words. Afterwards, repeat the second part of the sentence together as the child performs the motions with you.

Motions to Use

...starts the day with a walk.

 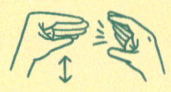

...meet, rub heads, and talk.

...run, jump, and play.

Slap knees on a flat surface, striking one palm after another in a walking motion. If standing, stomp the floor with alternating feet.

Form two fists, bringing each together to meet. Twist them against each other to "rub heads," then open and close fingers and thumb to "talk."

"Run" fingers over lap. Slap lap with quick rises to "jump." Clap once for "play."

...eat to be strong each day.

Raise hand to mouth as though holding a fork, pretending to eat. Flex your muscles.

...learn how to roar!

Open both hands, thrust them forward, and roar loudly.

...watch the birds that soar.

Make your hands fly like a bird.

...hear their mother's call.

Put a hand to your ear.

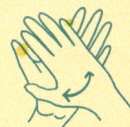 

...take a bath before nightfall.

Rub hands and arms to wash. Slowly lower hands to lap to signify "nightfall".

...curl up to go to sleep.

Cross arms. Raise folded arms to cheek as though they are a pillow.

Ten Tough Little Tigers...

Hold up 10 fingers.

...too tired to make a peep.

Hold one finger up to your mouth in a "shh" motion.

About the Author

A highly regarded member of the Florida Keys Writers Guild, Norma's talents were put to good use while playing with her grandchildren and their friends. Together, they would set up imaginary environments where collectable bears were given names like people. She coined the term *imagineering* to describe this activity. Creating stories with them as they played and breathing life into the bears, she taught life lessons while entertaining their imagination. Over time she would write the stories and send them as gifts to each of the children. She inspired the children to go on to write their own stories. To this day, the children still remark of holding on dearly to those pages laced with life lessons and sprinkled with love.

www.ingramcontent.com/pod-product-compliance
Lightning Source LLC
Chambersburg PA
CBHW040724060526
44119CB00083B/316